001

002

003

004

My heart is lone,
For you 'tis sad,
Give me your own,
And make it glad.

TO MY VALENTINE

005

I AM YOURS

006

To one, I Love

007

My Heart's best Gift.

008

To My VALENTINE

My Heart beats warm,
as warm can be,
And this is 'cause
of loving thee.

009

A Valentine for MY TEACHER

010

A token of Affection

011

DON'T "DODGE" ME BE MY VALENTINE

012

Can't You See I Love You?

013

TO MY VALENTINE

014

To greet My Love

015

The music of your voice
Just makes my heart rejoice,
For I know that
You are mine,
My own sweet
Valentine.

016

To my Valentine

017

To My Valentine

018

019

To my
Valentine

Cupid shot straight when he used the dart
That shot your image straight to my heart.

020

I came to
inquire,
if you found
a little heart
That perhaps
belonged
to me."

ST. VALENTINE'S GREETING

021

To One
I Love

022

To My Valentine

023

If I could catch YOUR HEART DEAR VALENTINE I'd throw the others back

024

MY VALENTINE!

I'D LIKE TO "RUNABOUT" WITH YOU!

025

LOVING GREETING

026

027

HiYA, Sugar
You're some DISH!

028

LET ME BE
YOUR
PET!
VALENTINE

029

TO MY
LITTLE
SWEETHEART

030

With
Love's
Greeting.

031

032

Tho' Cupid's dart has reached my heart, And pierced it through and through; I did not mind sweet Valentine, Because it came from you.

033

034

Be Mine

To My Valentine

035

036

THINK of Me!

037

My Valentine think of me.

038

TO MY VALENTINE

BE MINE

YOU'RE "TOPS"

039

AINT I ALWAYS TELLING YOU I LOVE YOU?

040

041

042

043

044

045

046

047

048

049

050

YOU'RE NICE TO CUDDLE Valentine

051

Hi, Valentine!

How's Tricks?

052

053

054

My
Love
to
You.

055

My
Heart's
best
Gift.

056

TO MY
LOVE

057

Cupid will tell
you plain and true,
No other maid
I love but you.

TO MY
VALENTINE

058

Sweet Valentine

MADE IN U.S.A.

059

VALENTINE
GREETINGS
TO
MY SWEETHEART

060

To fall out
of love is simply awful.

SER 404

061

WANT ANY HELP, GEORGE?

062

To My Valentine

063

CUPID being asked one day
True Beauty to define,
With magic touches He produced
Your Portrait,
VALENTINE.

COPYRIGHT 1909 R. WESSLER

064

A Gift of Love

065

Valentine Greetings

066

067

068

069

070

071

072

073

From your Valentine.

074

075

076

077

079

078

080

081

082

083

084

085

086

089

087

088

090

Joy and Pleasure be Yours

091

092

093

094

Accept this loving
heart of mine,
And be my own true Valentine.

Love's
Greeting

095

096

To my
VALENTINE.

Dan Cupid
badly wants to know
Whether you like the rings below—
This style,
or somewhere near it.
And then there's just
one other thing,
And that is—
when I buy
the ring,
Will you
agree
to wear it?

097

ROSES ARE RED
VIOLETS ARE BLUE
I'LL ALWAYS BE WARMHEARTED TOWARD YOU

098

Greeting to my
little sweetheart.

099

JUST TO SHOW
MY LOVE

100

101

102

103

104

105

106

107

Be my Valentine

I'm strong for you

108

109

YOU'VE SWEPT ME OFF MY FEET

110

111

I'm ready for the bridal path, Dear Valentine

112

113

114

115

116

117

118

119

Caught at last!

120

121

I Know You Like A Book My Valentine

122

123

To my Little Valentine with Love from you know whom

124

To my Valentine

125

A Valentine
MAIL
BE MINE

126

Our hearts, my Love, were formed to be
The genuine twins of sympathy,
They live with one sensation.
In joy or grief, but most in love,
Like chords in unison they move
And thrill with like vibration.

127

TO MY VALENTINE MOTHER

128

129

130

THIS
VALENTINE
BRINGS MY HEART
TO YOU
YOU'LL FIND IT
FAITHFUL, WARM
AND TRUE

131

132

Cupid's watching 'round your home,
To show this heart of mine,
And give to you this message,
"Please be my Valentine."

To My Valentine

133

Love's fond Message.

134

Valentine Greetings

To my Valentine

MADE in GERMANY
H.B.

135

TO MY
VALENTINE

136

To my
Valentine

GERMANY.

137

OF ALL THE BOYS
I E'ER DID SEE
YOU ARE THE
ONE MOST
DEAR TO
ME.

139

A VALENTINE
FOR MY TEACHER

This Valentine
Brings happy thoughts
To a teacher whom I like
JUST LOTS.

138

MY HEART IS SWEET FOR A SWEET VALENTINE

LIKE YOU!

140

Love's fond Greeting.

141

Love's fond Message

Call Cupid to your aid,
my dear,
And send me just a line,
To say, that whether
far or near,
You will be
always mine.

142

I'm WORRIED! Will YOU Be mine?

143

I'M NOT "KITTEN"... I REALLY WANT YOU FOR MY Valentine!

144

To my best Love.

145

146

147

148

149

150

151

152

153

154

155

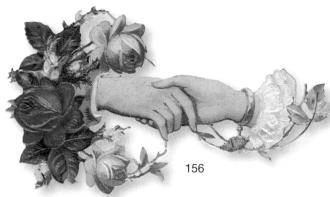

156

157

158

159

160

My
Love
think
of Me.

I'm
wholly
thine, my
Valentine.

161

Dearest,
be true,
as I'm to you.

To my
Valentine.

162

LOVING
THOUGHTS

OF
YOU

DEAR
VALENTINE

I

LOVE

YOU

163

164

Valentine's Plea

Your voice in laughter or in Song,
Holds in its spell the whole day long
One who would say "The world is mine!
If you would be my Valentine."

165

Come, be my little sweetheart,
Let joy in your eyes shine,
Accept this little token
From your own Valentine.

With Love's Greeting.

166

167

A
VALENTINE
MESSAGE

168

Loving Thoughts

169

170

St.
Valentine's
Greeting.

Thy charms are many, my merits few,
Yet I venture to offer my heart to you

171

172

173

174

175

176

177

178

179

180

181

182

183

A Token of Love.

I'll have no Valentine but you,
Be mine, Sweetheart, and aye be true!

184

185

186

187

188

189

To my Valentine.

190

191

STOP YOUR HOWLING OF COURSE I WANT YOU FOR MY VALENTINE

192

To My Valentine

CUPID'S been out shooting, and
His bag is very fine;
So should he call and offer you
That little **HEART** of mine,
I hope that you will keep it:
For my sake Sweet **VALENTINE**

193

194

To the
one I love.

195

To
my
Valentine

196

197

Love's
fond Gift.

198

Cupid's
Offering
To You

TO MY
VALENTINE

199

This bow of Green,
Fulfills Love's dream
I send it unto thee
And Hope that
You my Valentine
May be

love

200

Will
you

be my Valentine?

201

202

203

204

205

206

207

In this small
sign I find
a way
To greet my
dearest
Love to-day.

To my Valentine.

210

208

209

211

212

FOR MY
VALENTINE

213

214

215

NOBODY'S DARLING BUT MINE.

216

217

218

With Love

To My Own Dear Valentine

MY HEART

If you collect
such stamps as these,
As long since I've
suspected;
I hope you'll prize
THIS ONE above
All others you've
collected.

219

To My Sweetheart From

220

221

222

Light of those eyes
that made
The light of mine,
My Valentine.

223

224

225

226

227

228

229

230

231

232

233

234

235

Dear
Valentine   I tell you
true
My heart beats fast
with love for you

236

'TWOULD
GIVE ME
GREAT
PLEASURE
IF YOU'D
BE MY
TREASURE

MY
VALENTINE

237

I'LL SAY IT WITH MUSIC
I WANT YOU FOR MY VALENTINE

238

USE NO HOOKS FRAGILE
8,000,000 HEARTS
Handle with care

5¢ Valentine 5¢

Valentine Greetings

239